**Purchased with
Smart Start Funds**

CATS

MICHAELA MILLER

Contents

Heinemann Interactive Library
Des Plaines, Illinois

Wild Ones

Cats come in lots of different shapes and sizes. There are big wild cats like lions, tigers, and panthers and small cats that we keep as pets.

lioness with her cubs

But whatever they look like, they are all related to wild cats which first lived about twelve million years ago.

People first started keeping cats as pets about 4,000 years ago. They were used to catch the rats and mice that ate people's food.

gray tabby cat

Cats first came to the United States with the early settlers.

The Cat for You

There are long-haired cats and short-haired cats.

Long-haired cats need help to keep their fur clean and tidy. They must be combed and then brushed every day to keep them healthy. This can take a long time.

Persian cats

CAT FACT

A fluffy kitten will probably turn into a long-haired cat!

Short-haired cats look after their own fur by licking it with their rough tongues.

Where to Find Your Cat

Looking after a cat or a kitten is lots of fun. But it also takes lots of time and money. Before you get a cat, talk about it for a long time with your family. Make sure you can all look after a cat or kitten properly.

kittens in an animal shelter

There are lots of ways to find a cat or kitten. **Animal shelters** are often looking for good homes for cats. You could also ask a veterinarian.

kittens

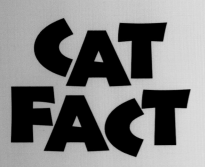

Kittens need lots of attention. They also need to be trained to use a litter box.

A Healthy Cat– What to Look for

The cat or kitten you choose should have a soft, smooth coat and clear, bright eyes. It should also have clean ears, a soft, clean nose, and a clean bottom.

A sneezing cat or one with a runny nose is probably not healthy. Don't take it home with you.

A healthy, happy cat or kitten enjoys playing.

9

Safe Hands

Cats and kittens usually love to be petted and held, but be gentle. Make friends slowly. Most cats like to be petted softly around the ears and chest, and around their neck and back.

When you are allowed to pick up your cat, pick it up very carefully with both hands and support its bottom and back legs.

CAT FACT

Holding on to a cat when it wants to get away will make it unhappy.

11

Feeding Time

Cats need two or three small meals a day at regular times. Kittens need about three or four even smaller meals. Pet supply stores and supermarkets sell cat food. Read the labels on the cat food carefully. Look for **vitamins** and **minerals**.

CAT FACT

Dog food should not be given to cats or kittens. It doesn't have all the right vitamins and minerals to keep them healthy.

You will need a bowl for food and a bowl for water. The bowls should be washed carefully after each meal.

Home Sweet Home

Your cat will need a clean, quiet place like a basket or a box where it can sleep. It will also need a **litter box** where it can go to the bathroom.

The litter box must be cleaned at least once a day. It is best to keep your cat inside to protect it from accidents and disease. Indoor cats are healthier, safer, and live longer.

Cats can sleep between sixteen and eighteen hours a day.

Keeping Clean

Cats are very clean. Your cat will spend a lot of time washing and **grooming**, so it won't need a regular bath. But it will probably like to be groomed gently by you with a soft brush.

mother cat grooming her kitten

Cats can get worms which live in their stomachs and make them sick. Take your cat to the veterinarian if it has worms.

You will need to check your cat for fleas. Fleas can live on the cat, bite it, and make its skin itchy. If your cat has fleas, the veterinarian can suggest something to get rid of them.

17

At the Veterinarian

Besides you, a veterinarian is your cat's best friend. When you get your new cat take it to the veterinarian for a checkup. The veterinarian will say when your cat should have **shots** to stop it from catching diseases.

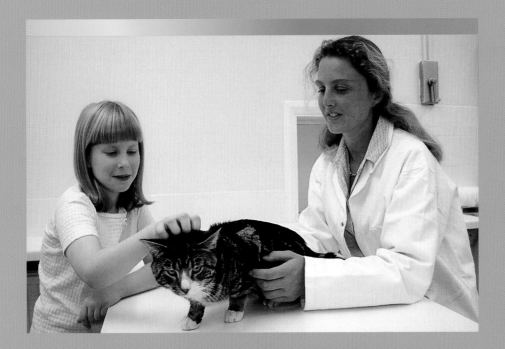

These shots are usually done once a year with a regular checkup and are very important. They could save your cat's life and also stop diseases spreading to other cats and kittens.

To find the name of a local veterinarian, look in the Yellow Pages or ask friends who have pets.

No More Kittens

There are many unwanted cats and kittens in the world and not enough people to take care of them. Don't let your cat–male or female–add to the problem. Your veterinarian can tell you how **neutering** will help.

CAT FACT

A female cat that has not been neutered can have up to three litters of kittens a year, with five kittens in each litter.

mother feeding her young

Lots of owners find that their male cats are much easier to live with when they have been neutered. It stops them wandering off and fighting. Female cats will not have kittens if they have been neutered.

A Note From the ASPCA

Pets are often our good friends for the very best of reasons. They don't care how we look, how we dress, or who our friends are. They like us because we are nice to them and take care of them. That's what being friends is all about.

This book has given you information to help you know what your pet needs. Learn all you can from this book and others, and from people who know about animals, such as veterinarians and workers at animal shelters like the ASPCA. You will soon become your pet's most important friend.

MORE BOOKS TO READ

Fowler, Allan. *It Could Still be a Cat.* Columbus Ohio: Childrens Press, 1993.

Kalman, Bobbie and Tammie Events. *Little Cats.* New York: Crabtree Publishing Co., 1994.

Glossary

When words in this book are in bold, **like this,** they are explained in this glossary.

animal shelters There are many of these shelters all around the country that look after unwanted pets and try to find them new homes.

grooming This means brushing and combing your cat.

litter box This is a box where a cat can go to the bathroom. It can be filled with soil or with special material called litter.

neutering This is an operation to stop cats from being able to have kittens.

shots Cats have to have shots from a veterinarian to stop them catching diseases.

vitamins and minerals Most foods contain vitamins and minerals. A good diet will have enough of the right vitamins and minerals to keep an animal healthy.

Index

Published by Heinemann Interactive Library, an imprint of Reed Educational & Professional Publishing,
1350 East Touhy Avenue, Suite 240 West, Des Plaines, IL 60018
© 1998 RSPCA

Produced by Times Offset (M) Sdn. Bhd.
Designed by Nicki Wise and Lisa Nutt
Illustrations by Michael Strand

02 01 00 99
10 9 8 7 6 5 4 3 2

Library of Congress Cataloging-in-Publication Data
Miller, Michaela, 1961-
　Cats / Michaela Miller.
　p. cm. — (Pets)
　Includes bibliographical reference and index.
　Summary: A simple introduction to choosing and caring for a cat.
　ISBN 1-57572-572-X (lib. bdg.)
　1. Cats — Juvenile literature. [1. Cats. 2. Pets.] 1. Title.
II. Series: Miller, Michaela. 1961- Pets.
SF445.7.M55 1998 　　　　　　　　　　　97-16614
636.8'083—dc21 　　　　　　　　　　　CIP
　　　　　　　　　　　　　　　　　　　AC

Acknowledgments
The author and publishers are grateful to the following for permission to reproduce copyright photographs.
Dave Bradford pp3, 5, 8-15, 17; Bruce Coleman Ltd/ p21 Jane Burton; RSPCA/ p2 Julie Meech,
p6 Colin Seddon, pp4, 7 E A Janes, pp16, 20 Angela Hampton, pp18, 19 Tim Sambrook.
Cover photographs reproduced with permission of: RSPCA; Dave Bradford
With special thanks to the ASPCA and their consultant Dr. Stephen Zawistowski, who approved the contents of this book.
Every effort has been made to contact copyright holders of any material reproduced in this book.
Any omissions will be rectified in subsequent printings if notice is given to the publisher.